MY STU

MY STUDIO

POEMS

Clarence Major

LOUISIANA STATE UNIVERSITY PRESS

BATON ROUGE

Published by Louisiana State University Press
Manufactured in the United States of America
First printing

DESIGNER: Mandy McDonald Scallan
TYPEFACE: Apollo
PRINTER AND BINDER: LSI

Grateful acknowledgment is extended to the following journals in
which some of these poems also appeared:

The Baffler: "The Spoon" and "The Story"; *Boulevard:* "May Day";
Catamaran Magazine: "Consider" and "The Cycle"; *Hambone:*
"Bowling Ball" and "Music Therapy; *Peacock Journal:* "Regenerative
Forces," "Undulating Contours," "Aesthetic Debt," "Home," and
"Vantage Point."

Library of Congress Cataloging-in-Publication Data
Names: Major, Clarence, author.
Title: My studio : poems / Clarence Major.
Description: Baton Rouge : Louisiana State University Press, [2018]
Identifiers: LCCN 2017055807 | ISBN 978-0-8071-6900-1 (pbk. : alk.
paper) | ISBN
   978-0-8071-6901-8 (pdf) | ISBN 978-0-8071-6902-5 (epub)
Classification: LCC PS3563.A39 A6 2018 | DDC 811/.54—dc23
LC record available at https://lccn.loc.gov/2017055807

CONTENTS

Vantage Point — 1

Van Gogh's Chair — 2

Undulating Contours — 4

The Tuffet and the Spider — 6

The Story — 7

The Spoon — 8

Relocating Beavers — 9

Regenerative Forces — 11

Pursuit — 12

Perception — 13

Home — 14

Fruitfulness — 16

Enthusiasm — 18

Common Sense — 19

Aesthetic Debt — 20

A Rhapsody — 21

A Modest Dream — 22

A Malleable Night — 24

A Tragedy Indisputable — 25

The List — 26

Morocco — 27

May Day — 28

Frequency — 29

Consider — 30

Conjuring for Rain — 31

Burnt Orange — 32

By a Venice Alley — 33

Angels — 35

Dürer's *Young Couple Threatened by Death* — 37

Numbers — 38

Elevated — 40

Emily Dickinson — 41

Nimbus — 43

The Fight — 45

Tracing — 47

Afternoon Rain — 49

Inspiration — 50

Kissing Cousins — 51

Opera — 52

Still Life — 54

A Walk in the Park — 56

An Incalculable Process — 57

Assertion — 58

Everyday Objects — 59

Dead Birds — 61

Music Therapy — 63

Oak Trees — 65

Seedlings — 67

Bowling Ball — 69

Mother's Rain — 70

The Tour — 71

The Summit — 72

Salute — 73

Possibilities — 74

The Revelation — 75

A French Machete — 76

A Byzantine Moment — 77

Eye Wash — 78

My Studio — 81

MY STUDIO

Vantage Point

It's a peculiar inwardness,
as mysterious as the Baltic Sea is to me.
But I'm utterly free
to be carefree and transfixed.

What I meant to say is
I love the slope of the tree line,
the wind-tossed leaves
leaving the trees
like blind birds
and the jutting crags seeming to
crawl the earth.

From my vantage point—a gully
on a hillside, where I clip-clip-clip
as two seagulls watch, waiting.

The fraternity
of nature's secrets enthralls!
The wonderments!
The wonderments!

I marvel
at the scattering of new growth.
I'm here
where all the parts coalesce
into a cohesive whole.

Van Gogh's Chair

As a project to challenge myself,
I set the task of duplicating
van Gogh's simple chair—
simple compared to Gauguin's
more elaborate armchair.

I waxed my saw table, set my blade
perfectly vertical with the surface.

I used the dowel
to make sure the blade
and the slots were parallel.

I tested everything
to make sure everything
was working properly.

The saw was in alignment.
With knightly loyalty to the task,
I was fortified with creative energy.

As I shaped the long back legs,
the short front legs, the back
support frame, the eight spokes,
I kept the saw free of sawdust,
gum and pitch,
brushing the waste to the floor.

My table-tools and supplies were simple:
gage, wrench, arbor nut, push stick,
glue, staples, screwdriver, and straightedge.

I was careful to guard against kickback.
Then I weaved the straw seat—
getting it much like the original.

After three days
of constant work, fitting and gluing,
there it was, standing in my workshop,
unpretentious, a thing of verisimilitude,
lacking ornamentation,

yet a thing of unprecedented brightness,
a yellow van Gogh chair,
radically simplified,
unintimidating—a worthy subject.

Undulating Contours

We're both bourgeois audience
and performance.
We live with the dominance
of a certain tendency.

Yet we long for a joyous communion.
No doubt about it.
We're headed to a blurred indefinite place.

Not that we want to go.
We certainly don't fully believe
in its prospects.

The garbage truck comes.
Half the garbage is left in the can.

I ask what's the context of the climate.
Yes, there's a dominance
of a certain tendency.
It has become a rigid mission.

But not *all* is lost.
We make peace with our forebodings.
We love old movie posters and film noir.
We love trees reflected in water.
Shimmering, they somehow look coquettish.
We still read George Orwell.
We read Conrad too.
We watch voyeuristic melodramas.
We love silent cinema and the color mauve.
We say freedom, not emancipation.

Meanwhile, high in the hills above our city:
secret carvings on boulders.
We are struggling to understand them.
If we have the discipline
they may redefine us—for the better.

The Tuffet and the Spider

She sat on her tuffet stool
(to her father, a footstool.)
She loved its shifting contours,
its profusion of pleats fascinated her.
She loved its shimmering reds
and greens and silky texture.

As she was finishing her cornflakes,
a big green spider dropped down
from the chandelier to her lap.

And that was the beginning
of another story's ending,
a story in which snapdragons
were always available
to eat stray spiders
despite the bad taste.

It was the kind of love story,
in which love is best achieved
by giving assiduously.

The Story

The story involves fireworks on display,
day lilies in bloom,

also an unhappy doomed stepdaughter,
nymphs playing in the fountain,

a mysterious trip
to Tangier as a place of refuge,

a priceless painting
once owned by Durand-Ruel,

a strange odor
at the local flax market,

Monet's old dried-up paint tubes,
an ill-matched couple
from Finland on their honeymoon,
the town prostitute

with a new umbrella and new shoes,
a diary someone kept

while visiting Mesopotamia,
Cyrus the Great ordering

the rebuilding of the Temple,
Marcel Proust's mattress

with his body-print still in it,
and Napoleon's tongue.

But don't worry.
I won't tell you the ending.

You'll be surprised.

The Spoon

So the dish ran away with the spoon.
Although the dish prevailed,
what they didn't tell us is
how the spoon escaped.

The spoon wanted more contrast.
That's a fact. It's also a fact
that juxtapositions are endless—

frying pans and bricks,
skillets and hammers,
the fluttering flags of small nations
and old books with titles printed in gold,
a shrine of three crosses

and used tablecloths,
family photographs badly faded
and benches with three legs,
frayed Indian rugs

and the remains of a stone terrace
and broken plates,
wrenches and nametags
and a pile of pine bark
and pigeon feathers.

Each has its contrasting harmony,
as with Cézanne's apples and jugs.
Also, as with Cézanne,
if you don't know what goes
with what, you leave it alone.

Relocating Beavers

We all knew our lake was overrun
with beavers.

Decisive park officials trapped
and put them on a helicopter.

As a volunteer, I went with them.
We airlifted and flew them
to a remote mountain area.

Then they were parachute-dropped
into dense wooded foothills
near a mountain lake.

There is nothing surprising in the fact
that the beavers objected.
They're known to complain a lot.

The earth shook and trembled
when they landed.
They landed like symbols
falling into mythologies.

I saw them scatter,
some running off into a thicket
of mystic roses.

Anyway, the area was annexed
to the cave where Cinderella
(long ago) was held captive.

I saw two beavers run
straight for that cave.

Within seconds they reemerged
as two galloping white horses.

And they took off for the sky,
disappearing into the clouds—

beavers defying relocation.

Regenerative Forces

I'm at the summit.
I've so far managed to elude the rules.

I was told yesterday to watch out
up here for a culmination.

So far, only an eruption has taken place.
I know, I know. I need to elucidate.

But so much remains marginal.
That is the problem with fluid elements.

Up here, so high up,
nightmares easily become daydreams.

Multifaceted problems melt into one.
Oh, I forgot to tell you.

I'm wearing a farmer's smock.
I'm pretty sure nobody so far recognizes me.

I'm forging a new identity.

Pursuit

I'm the absolute protagonist.
I'm taking a vertiginous viewpoint here.
We're in a gin joint of the 1920s.

A lot of dancing
and playful grasping.

I'm depending on dynamism
to get me through.
If things go south
I can always escape
through the side door.

They got a board
nailed across the back door:
an interesting architectural detail.

But don't get the idea
that there is no aesthetic progress.
It's codified!

And the press wants to know everything we do.
Listen to the shutters clicking.
Click-click, click-click!

Perception

If the cow jumped over the moon
(in her terrain of gravity)

what on earth is left
for the cow to accomplish?

I assume she does not live by symbols.
Like many of us,

she is still in an unresolved descent.
Her view is slanted

and from where I watch
her aloof profile and our gaze,

there is, on our part, an erosion of trust,
replaced by a branded defiance.
Even watching through a wide-angle lens,
not everyone watching

appreciates the spatial depth
of her (or our) experience.

Now we await the appraisal.

Home

My first home, long ago:
situated in a timeless harbor.

Never mind the resonant light—
its surest metaphor.

A compelling seriousness
served a massive stillness

rooted in majestic sobriety.
I grew up innocenct and aware,

with three glories—
faith, hope, and charity.

And grew out of glory
into understanding—
not *with*standing.
But the question is:

can I return to the idea
or would I want to?

To return to an inherited place . . .
To return to a place

of negotiated surfaces . . .
Grimly exacting, though

structured for flexibility.
Is it necessary to re-embrace it,

to re-embrace the concept
or circumstances?

Its light shines on
with single-mindedness:
a conceptual paradox.
Now the stillness has given way

to an annoying clamor
and to inexact memory;

and that is a home
I no longer need

but can't give up.

Fruitfulness

The bullring was circular,
the cape square,
both for good reasons.

Relatives tried to make me take things
in my right hand.
I refused.
I had my reasons.

I was whirling in an allegory
of turbulent earth and skies.
Ubiquitous,
my left hand had power of attorney.
It was fortified,
held in repeating synthesis.

(But mother never had a problem
with my left hand.

It was a kind of moat,
a bridge, she could cross and re-cross,
it was also a furrow.)

Yet in this right-handed world,
I remained both exposed and undisclosed,
atypical,
surrounded by an aura
of haughtiness and odd happiness.

I was constantly negotiating curves,
defending sketchy strokes,
avoiding curious people, making risky friends.

(Jimmy held his scotch glass
in his left hand. So I was in good company.)

But generally and unfortunately
the left hand made polite company
uneasy.

In certain countries
people thought it was crude
to use it to eat.
It was for wiping yourself.

I saw the diagonal swing of it.
I extended it, tower-like,
much like the Leaning Tower of Pisa.

My hand was a dangling branch
swinging against the current,
a branch heavy with fruitfulness.

Enthusiasm

Standing on one leg,
we endured the miner's strike,
the cries of the boy
as the country doctor
wrapped the broken leg,

the smell of the fish market,
peasants arguing politics,
lovers weeping on the bridge,
beggars on All Saints Day.

We endured riding bareback
to the watering hole,
the reading of the disappointing will.

We endured visiting day at the hospital,
the dead child in the casket.

Now look at those clowns
down the road and up the hill,
standing on one leg,
shouting, *"Hipp hipp hurra!"*

Common Sense

At thirteen I painted pictures
of fluttering flowers.
It took common sense to do that.
I was in control.

Years later—*many* years later—
I wanted to be immune to common sense,
to the ordinary,
to dullness, to fatigue,
to boredom, to paradox,
to uninteresting ever-present common sense.

To map my future
(and forgive my past)
I used an energetic template of creativity.
I was like a Greek hero with mythical sirens
swimming circles around me.

They were the cause
of raucous excitement.
But common sense followed me
with its humanist agenda.

I was suspended
between yin and yang.
To escape the answerless void,

I sought shelter in the elegant dignity
of my own imagination,
and there I found fluorescent-lit questions
more interesting than answers—
many so predictable.

Aesthetic Debt

We leave the casino in Monte Carlo.
A ship anchored in calm water.
In a generous gesture,
we suspend our sense of rootedness.
Should art always give pleasure?

What of the natural discourse
between art and the recipient,
the radical highlights,
the dismantled reverence,
religious reverence,
graphic turmoil?

Art is there, waiting.
It forgives a whole town hall of mistakes.
We arrive
with outstanding aesthetic debt.
To say nothing
of harmful critical judgment,
even critical prejudice.
Illuminations are flickering, flickering—
light through porous paper.

I study a lithographic stone
glowing in the dark.
The artist says it is art.
We come out in the open
where elephants are sunbathing.

A Rhapsody

I slipped my feet into unidentified shoes.
The comfort scared me.
When I tried to take them off I could not.

Provocative bait, they changed my plans.
They led me through debauchery to poverty.
I lost my gait and slept in a quarry in the woods.

On crossbars I was hooked and double-crossed.
I was out of orbit, sleeping in opaque farmhouses.

Fed up, broke, ill, and depressed,
unregistered, unfortified yet intransigent,
I bid the shoes to take me home.

You can imagine the extravagant outcome.
They took me deeper into the irredeemable.

Then, by accident, they led me home.
But home had become a series of windows
with heartbroken faces classic with grief.

A Modest Dream

I wanted to sit in the coolness of a patio
and write poems.
But I had no patio.

So, with a naturalist vision
and with a reservoir of architectural ideas,
I decided to build one—a great one.

At City Hall I got a permit then set to work.
Working from a rough thumbnail,
I poured a concrete slab.

I bought posts, lumber for floorboards,
railings, wood for steps, spokes, etc.

To keep them parallel and aligned,
I nailed cleats to the posts.

The patio represented a certain aesthetic
with cornerstones
paying allegiance to art.

The whole effect was synonymous
with the highest ideals of beauty.

I hammered and fitted,
hammered and fitted
till the patio was finished.

Finished,
I sat with my computer on my lap,
looking out at the backyard.

Birds and insects
visited the area frequently.
Unusual birds
(*even hummingbirds!*) and insects
kept coming.

After several months of effort at poetry
on the patio
I realized the *patio* was my poem.

A Malleable Night

That night nobody cared
that debris was left in the sink.
The toilet bowl and the sink were broken.
People went next door.

We lived up the street.
To get there was a ten-minute walk.
Eddie lived across the street from the tavern.

Sadie didn't mind the foot traffic.
The refrigerator was off balance and off-limits.

(Havelock Ellis said love was an art.)

Eddie got up on the stage with his saxophone.
You could tell, he was in love.
Everybody came to have a good time.
They were letting the "good times roll."

Yes, Eddie was deeply in love.
Shouting: *"It was when my baby left me
that I sat right down and cried."*

And everybody was on his side:
"She just threw away a good man!"

A Tragedy Indisputable

Sunday night
they held a funeral for him.

The preacher, against strong backlighting,
sounded a resonant note.

(The boy's death diabolical and macabre
and now his mangled body

disfigured
lay in a casket before us . . .)

So many people
they couldn't all get in the church.

Our allegiance to logic and reason
now in perpetual sway

and we are circumspect in every step.
No judicious recovery in sight . . .

Hundreds stood out on the sidewalk
listening to the preacher's voice

through the loudspeaker.
Our much-adored progeny

struck down
by vulgar bigotry . . . and no amount

of inquisitiveness
can explain to us the hideous cult

of murder in the woods.

The List

All shot. Shot many times!
Many, many times!
Dying on the street. On the street!
Dying at the bottom of steps.

Shot in bed. In bed!
Shot in toilets. In toilets!
Shot in the subway. In the subway!

Shot on the side of the road.
Shot with witnesses all around.
Shot with no witnesses around.

Shot in the back nine times. In the back!
Shot in the face nine times. In the face!
Shot again and again in the back.

Shot again and again in the face. In the face!
Shot forty times in a doorway. In a doorway!
Shot in cars. Shot beside cars. Shot behind cars.

Shot. Shot. Shot. Shot.

Morocco

Eighty miles west of here
goats are up in trees
eating argan nuts.

When they poop the kernels out
farm workers collect them.

In our medicine cabinet
my wife has a bottle of oil
from those kernels.

Says it's good for her skin.

So we thank the trees.
And we thank the goats.
The system is working.

May Day

On May Day
a friend says he is about to become homeless.
He is distressed and needs help.
His problem is he can't live
anywhere near people.

At night he becomes two people.
In the loudest possible voice,
one self-cross-examines the other.

The interrogation is electric.
Done harshly, with pomp and ceremony.
You would think Joan of Arc was on trial.
(*He* would say Jeanne d'Arc.)
And he does it every night.
Neighbors hear through walls.
They complain.
At first he's recalcitrant.
He feels he's the victim of recriminations.

He's given notice.
He feels defenseless.
He can't make the fervent appeal that he feels.
There's nothing to fortify him
against the impending disaster.

Someone suggested he go to the cemetery
to do his cross-examination.
The dead can't hear.
Creatures of rigid formality,
they are circumspect, patient, and kindly.
They tolerate just about anything—even
a man in two parts
cross-examining himself
in a voice of fire and brimstone.

Frequency

I like an Intended who arrives
with a dowry of kindness and loyalty.

I like indeterminacy gauged
by the difficult frequency
of certainty rumbling loudly.

I like sharp edges gauged by soft edges.

I like a watershed moment
that comes after much sincere effort.

I like hotel lobbies filled with dancing skeletons.

On the other hand, I embrace the unknown.

I embrace interesting silhouettes
in any unique atmosphere.

I embrace any fervent commitment
to a good cause.

I embrace self-reliance.

But most of all
I embrace an allegory
of luminous love,
expressed under turbulent skies,
on a Japanese footbridge
over a water garden
with afternoon sunlight
shifting delicately down
through
the surrounding cherry trees
in bloom.

Consider

Dearly beloved, if you like, call this an allegory.
One is implicated when one picks up the brush.
A subjective and eminently modern question:
Problem of subject matter!
Start up the ladder or start anywhere.
Consider the girl with bed-head hair.

Consider the Apocalypse in smoke.
Consider Tanner at his easel.
Consider the solicitous suitor.
On his knees before the vivacious girl!
She loves the Russian Ballet—nineteenth-century version.
Consider her humor and zest.

Consider the girl wearing a gold-trimmed cloak:
Consider the left eye bigger than the right!
Consider Cézanne's freshly cut carrot.
He says it can start a revolution.
Revolution means rotation—progress in an orbit.
Find an orbit in an apple, in a roundabout.

Or in that mahogany tea table!
Consider Bonnard's mistress, Renee:
Consider the grief of Renee—dead in a hotel room.
Or consider a bar full of rowdy men drinking beer.
You are implicated from the start.
So you must make progress in that orbit!

Conjuring for Rain

At first we didn't know
the magnitude of the situation.

Previous flourishing had come to an end.
No rain for a whole year.

Grass died, trees drooped, bushes shriveled.
Temperaments withered.

I took to wearing a tarred oilskin.
I walked the streets ringing a bell.

I consulted fertility rain figurines.
No luck. No grapes to raisins.

I unfurled our sails to no avail.
I pulled on the pulley-rope to see if anything would fall.

We were at drought's mercy.
Our Garden of Eden was now exposed as floral-less.

The situation was irremediable.
The summarily rendered elegance of life passed.

No drought dependability!
Even the chrysanthemums in a jar died.

Burnt Orange

I'm in the car reading poetry.
I'm waiting for my wife.
She's in the post office.

The solitude of crows nesting in palm trees.
An indecisive pigeon high on a ledge.
The ex-poet in an Ethiopian café eating spicy soup.
The hammer's sympathy for the nail.
The chatter of ghosts in the bedroom.

The sky is a clear light blue.
I wish I had the color burnt orange
to hold up next to it.

By a Venice Alley

I'm at a table out front

of my favorite little café,

enjoying an espresso.

Across the way,

a fogged-in enclave.

A pole handrail

to a steep narrow stairway

in a corner

to the left of a vaulted window

looking out

onto a lighted hallway

of cloistered air.

Elongated arches and pillars.

Stained-glass windows.

On a clear day from here,

a view of the sea.

Women on low stools

against the wall

in the coolness of shade

calmly stringing beads.

Across from me,

a dancer dancing

across a marble floor.

She twirls her arms

above her head and

from side to side.

When I left the cup

even the liquid of my espresso

seems to dance in rhythm

with the twirling,

then again

with those busy fingers

stringing beads.

Angels

My three-year-old sister

insists that angels in the backayrd

in long white robes

are surrounding her.

Constructed with inherent accuracy,

their wings lift up

from their shoulders

through openings in their robes.

Normally,

creatures of lyrical asceticism,

her angels are barefoot

and suspended a foot or two

off the earth

as they surround her,

waiting for her

to state her case.

I've been reading Schopenhauer

and privately

have an uncompromising view

of such matters;

but who am I

to argue with her

as she descends the back steps

into the backyard

holding her tiny pink parasol?

Dürer's *Young Couple Threatened by Death*

We shared the authority
of an honorable shame.
You, my Charlotte, I praised you.

I left for Portugal
and the Aegean Sea.
While away, I recognized your bait—
which was also my own.

You sat on my knee
and played your lute
and never fell into disrepute.

Returning,
I saw your virtues up close.
I dreamed we sailed
the Mediterranean together.

Our pleasures were augmented.
And by neighbors resented.

(We found a grape
behind Dürer's "Young Couple."
Together we touched history.)

But by defecting attention
it came to you more abundantly.
I was your boyfriend.
I was your decoy.
Ah, my sweetheart, I was your toy!

Numbers

Skin glued to flesh.

Skin falling away from flesh.

From now on, I will take no more.

I want no eye for an eye.

I see the sacred and the con artist

coming out the same cathedral door.

Tit for tat they say

and with an accent.

Eleven, innocent eleven,

condemned for excess.

Eleven exceeds perfection.

If ten is perfection

who will win next?

And why is winning the issue?

The clock is turning

Backwards, counter-clockwise,

retracing its' tick-tocking steps.

Antithesis: inversion and reversion.

But eleven wins in the end.

And this is the end.

Elevated

This is for you,
for your glory or amusement.
Although
it looks like fading realism,
it's a rhapsody that defies labeling.
I mean the elementary
and the simplicity of it.
The dependable certainty
of no clutter. No clutter!
A preparatory smile!
The boldness—the necessary thing.
A glowing bright yellow
against blue. Very blue!
A ship out at sea
at sunset.
Levitating!

Emily Dickinson

I try not to judge harshly, Emily,

remembering your

"Judge tenderly of me!"

But life is a one-legged beggar

carrying a knapsack

of broken promises.

Its true translation

is not possible.

Even as you speak of him:

"He ate and drank

the precious words"

uppermost in me.

Let the world be.

Though I write to her,

him and them,

I will never live

long enough to learn

their languages, Emily,

languages

that "never wrote to me."

Nimbus

At first it seems

to be a catastrophe,

something fallen

out of orbit—something

consumed by fire.

Then in time

no form is grounded

more firmly.

You can finally feel

the power thrashing—

like the very root

of fertility as the new

emerges (still blessed

with its halo)

from the hot ashes

of its old self.

Later, you can freely

smell its freshness,

like the smell

of wet evergreen

blooming.

As time passes

you can taste

the sweet, sweet air

it's burning and exhaling.

It's apocalyptic—indistructable.

It's reborn a better self.

Year after year it evolves.

It comes back fully,

with an insatiable appetite

for fruitfulness,

surprising you (and through

its renewal renewing you)

in season at each turn.

The Fight

We are breaching our contract.

When the verbal fight is over

the energy of its words

lingers in the air

like the loosen and flung feathers

of birds fighting in midair.

There are no heroes, no villians,

no legitimate squabbles

except perhaps those

of animals over territory.

It's like looking through a negative.

The outer edges shimmer.

What was invoked?

We can't remember.

The closer we move to the center

the more intense and agitated

the force;

those edges swirl around

like flying feathers

hitting a propeller.

And the two of us now

can't remember what we felt

so passionate about.

Tracing

Knowing she must choose

between wove and tracing,

impulsively

she chooses tracing.

Regretting her decision,

she stands by the stove

in self-derision.

The woes of paper!

So, for her it is see-through,

but she makes peace

with what is left:

pulp purple shadows,

and from up here in the air

she's tracing from trunk

to limb the trees,

and next morning

the road up to the house is wet

and transparently lovely

from night's rain and the sane air

is insanely fresh

as the paper-maker's inane blush.

Afternoon Rain

Morning fog lifted
from this windswept
pocket of land.

At shoreline wild roses
and cranberry bogs.

Remains of stress
from last week
when everything fell apart.

I walk to the inlet elbow
and sit on a sandy rock.

Out at sea tiny sails
floating like butterflies.

Last week:
Airplanes flying into buildings.
Thousands dying.

I pick up a whalebone fragment.
That same girl running
with her dog along the beach.

By noon it will begin
to cloud over.
The afternoon rain will come,
clearing by five.

The usual pattern.
But I'm not the same.

Inspiration

Thank you Rimbaud

the inimitable

my senses are reorganized

I'm ready to spend time

with those covered

in Vesuvius ash

or with Vuillard

looking into the mirror

at his own face

and seeing notations

not an image of himself

Kissing Cousins

She said let's go outside—
the night is beautiful.
We can celebrate your birthday.

The sky was full
of the tiny creatures of the night.
The twinkle of fireflies.
Yellow sparks in yellow eyes.

Suddenly my cousin kissed me,
as if I were the teddy
that slept on the pillow
next to her.

And I too glowed in the night.

Opera

When we lived in Venice

we suspended disbelief.

Opera was all the rage;

grief or comedy

night after night.

The smell of the presence

of lovely aromatic ladies of nobility.

On the stage in the end

Rosine and the Count marry.

Not much of a story line

yet the charm of innocent play

and aristocratic misdeeds

carry the day every night on stage.

Rossini took old stories

and retold them well, very well.

William Tell, William Tell

and *The Barber of Seville.*

Rossini wrote to Angelica

complaining

about the quality

of oysters in Rome,

but the ladies there

would not leave him alone,

while in Naples Angelica

ate fresh oysters every day.

Still Life

Night flowers not to be defeated.

We dance round the pond.

Cherry tree blossoms

around the pond

white blossoms bursting forth

announcing spring

above and below,

stars bright, undeleted.

Ducks in the pond quacking,

quacking

swimming round and round,

quacking.

We dance among the flowers,

happily, happily.

The chime of Dahlia-eye-music

in winter frost

dancing the dance of water lilies.

Chinese trees and the red flashlight

of Gladiolus

light the way

all the way around,

round the pond, stumble-free.

A Walk in the Park

Walking around the pond.
Clear sky with distant clouds
galloping off into the distance.

Water at last in the pond.
Ducks and egrets have come back.
They're swimming
on the mirror
of the brown water.

A duck lands with a crescendo.
Smell of oak and fern and lilac.

Pygmy shrubbery
lining the walkways.
Luxury houses
flanking the soccer field.
Lines of pine along the path.
The shrill *cheep cheep*
of small birds in the trees.

And the deep belch of ducks!
A stand of Chinese elm
juxtaposed to the lookout stand.

Benches, with names
of dead people,
all the way around!
We sit on Waldo's bench
for a few minutes.

Waldo died three years ago.
An engraved plaque:
"In loving memory of Waldo Glasgow."
Anne Glasgow.

An Incalculable Process

In the rain
she is already holding my hand.
The things she wants
are things I must learn.

Can she endure contradiction?
Does she like tragedy or comedy
or none of the above?
Does she want kids
or is she kidding?

Does she wear cotton or synthetics?
Does she dare?
Does she slough
or sit straight in a chair?
Will she say, "We will see,"
meaning "No way!"

Will she think a vegan diet
too bound, too geeky?
Is she afraid of clowns
and bored by fooling around?

Will we be able
to deal with the polarities?
Are there too many similarities?
When will I stop asking questions?
And when will she start?

Assertion

Put two things together:
see what you get.

Light and limerick
or liquor and lion.

In spheres of stardust
you find the rhythm, its' dance
before it finds language.

Plato says poetry stirs
the dullard to action,
makes him smarter.

There is a dance of life in it.
A waltz and then a foxtrot.
A foxtrot then the boogie-woogie.

Invisible touchstones *are* available.
There, greatness outshines greed.

Even when storms were eroding
the Royal Highway,
Gorky understood
more than he let on.

Everyday Objects

There is a certain magical beauty

in everyday things.

They contain a kind of spatula of play.

Among the permissible and impermissible

oddities *en masse:*

comfortable steering wheels,

eyeglass cases, paper towels,

non-messy fruitless trees,

tiny electric fans, doormats,

fruit jars to hold pencils,

easy-to-handle doorknobs,

bells that chime musically,

smoke detectors that work,

windows without drapes,

rugs from India, oak fences,

homes with plenty of books,

up-to-date computers;

and intangible things

such the visual glory of great art,

a sad lady singing the blues,

a great trumpeter making his horn talk,

the art of higher mathematics.

Ah, give me any nebula

of everyday magical beauty!

Dead Birds

Some things are temporary.
In grade school
we memorized:
the *Niña,* the *Pinta,*
and the *Santa María.*
George Washington Carver
and the peanut.

What is forgotten?
What is retained?
The brain knows
what's worth keeping.

So why did 18th-century
French painters
paint dead rabbits?
And dead birds
piled on the kitchen table.

Anyway, I love *un*even typeface.
Monotype Dante.
Easy to retain.
I also love the metamorphosis
of metamorphosis.

Even after burrowing inside
why, why remains elusive.
Memory dribbles,
wispy memory,
then there is its' paralysis.

Some things remain temporary,
wriggling (where they belong)
on the surface.
"Do you live in these parts?"
Weightless cargo.
Squid in a bucket!

Music Therapy

Something inside me
suddenly went wrong.
I felt remote—adrift on a skiff.
Two possibilities:
death or recovery.

Yet no expert knew the cause.
Had I tried hypnosis?
I lost patience being a patient.
Diagnosis came to nothing.
Doctrines and hypotheses
came to nothing.

Someone said
have you tried eminent utility:
otherwise known as medicine?

Though I was resolute
nothing worked.
I thought the trouble
might be my spleen.
The trouble might be my liver.

I concluded
my illness was arbitrary.
Something in my nature!
But Nature was also my caregiver.

And time—time both cared for
and ate away at me.
I drank liquids.
Swallowed pills.

My doctor said this will work
only if the problem
has a solution.
Better to have the trouble
on the surface of the skin.

Somebody said
music might help.
Imagine!
Music to alleviate suffering.
This attempt at a cure
seemed primitive.
Music might elevate
my mood or sooth me.
My goal was complete recovery.

Then the condition inside
went into remission.
Apparently, music worked
the illness to the surface.

Oak Trees

I feel at peace

among oak trees,

abetted by them.

Yet oak trees seem at times

to both fret at and to applaud

my presence.

I stop in the shadows

of a stand of California great oaks

in this temperate region

to pay allegiance.

Oak dominates here,

whispering gestural blessings

in a language I can hear

but cannot speak.

Eighty species of oak.

I know everything depends

on my understanding.

My breathing is their breathing.

And I hear the trees talking.

I learn languages quickly.

So I will soon speak their language.

Seedlings

I thought of writing a novel

like *Moll Flanders,*

but instead, I planted oleanders.

The oleanders alongside our fence

on the east side are now tall

as our second floor.

I thought of writing a novel

like *Maggie: A Girl of the Streets*

but instead sat in a lawn chair

and admired our oleanders.

Later, an oleander seedling

started growing in a flowerpot

I left in their shade.

I planted it on the south fence.

A seedling, beginning again

with fragile roots.

Perhaps in me a novel

also will grow from fragile roots

but for now

I'm father to oleander sprouts.

Bowling Ball

Centuries ago
it was done with gallantry.
The gods did it all the time.
Some were even petty
and malicious.

Nowadays participants
can be sultry and even
get your gall.

A hot day increases the chance
ready or not.

Some men carry that glow around
like a bowling ball.
And it misses as often.

A whole tribe never strayed
from that glowing way.
And now they are extinct.

My wife says there must be a link.

Mother's Rain

Just outside of Chicago
in the rain, I'm thinking
of Byron's grave of glory, as
the minster, carrying the iron cross,
passes the limousines
(passes the horses
moving in a thrashing circle)
up the hill of muddy tracks
toward the gravediggers
digging mother's grave

and I'm thinking it's so fitting
it should rain on the day
mother is lowered into the earth.
Her agony is over.
She would have chosen this, the rain.
She would have said this is my kind of day.

The Tour

You must go first
through an overgrown passageway

leading to the memorial
(to their founder)

by the marble action figure
(their war hero)

in front of the tall fountain
(to the flow of life)

with an occasional swan
swimming in it,

then sit
on the weathered wooden bench

against the stone wall
stained with moss

and wait for the ancient caretaker
to take you on the tour

but be forewarned
you don't come back

the same way
and you don't come back the same.

The Summit

We've too much stuff piling up,
a flourishing in successive places,

places unable to contain the stuff.
Stuff transmitted

from one unsuitable place
to another unsuitable place.

What is this fear of letting go,
of being overwhelmed?

What tenets drive this breach?
We say someday we might need . . .

But someday never comes.
It's self-deception. It's absurd.

We're eluding the rules of logic.
This is a domestic catastrophe,

perpetual eruptions.
We're suitable subject for lampooning,

even malicious caricature.
Our tendency fights our best judgment.

We say we are not hoarders.
We insist we are not hoarders.

Our accumulation isn't so hidden.
It's embarrassingly in the open.

It's continuous allusion to our illness.
Ah, where is the summit?

Salute

Last night wind galloped.
Rain beat the house
like a fool whipping a horse with a stick.

A tree in my neighbor's backyard
fell in the night into our backyard,
broke the fence,
but didn't damage our house.

Now the fallen tree is lying there
like a beached whale,
still breathing but faintly.

Although there is something
intimidating about it,
I have no anecdote,
no verbal excursion into why.
Can't say something was breached.

It's a beast with many naked winter-arms
saluting allegiance to something
beyond my ability to discern.

But something real is invoked
without elucidating its intention.

Nature's stronghold has its recruits,
its endless eruptions,
its marginal purposes,
its culminations and reconciliations.

And there is nothing we can do
but marvel at its multifaceted strategies;
and give a flourishing salute.

Possibilities

I think of Edward Hopper
and sunlight on a wall.

Where there is sunlight
there is also shade.

My farmhouse
throws a lot of shade across the yard.

Just beyond the sunlight
I study the shade's shifting contours.

This requires the fading of realism.
I feel free to doze off in the shade's solitude.

I remember the serenity of the shade.
Never mind the gloomy landscape

in which the farmhouse stands.
A bright moment given by sunlight!

I take it in, make it part
of my endless possibilities.

The Revelation

George Grosz said "a little yes" and a "big no."
For me it's a revelatory *yes* to a nihilistic *no.*

I comb nihilism from my nightmares.
I throw it overboard

down through dangling branches
into fluttering tides.

I am my own silent witness.
Although my abode is a place

of captivating grandeur,
I spend my time out in the open,

in the sunlight of *yes,*
in the clean geometry of nature.

I daydream, fascinated by
certain motifs for objects of desire.

They appear as both *yes* and *no.*
I'm hooked

like a Francophile at a French library.

A French Machete

I wake to the sounds of my neighbor,

the one-eyed farmer,

whose eye was picked out long ago

during the Algerian war.

I go to the window to see.

He's standing in the open field,

a reaper sharpening his machete

on a whetstone,

the *screech screech screech*

of the friction back and forth

(cutting across the provencial

morning silence of Nice)

with its brutal rhythm.

Well, if it's not him, it's the rooster.

A Byzantine Moment

Phillips' mistress is about to be married.
She's magnificent in her wedding gown
of medieval deep blues and bright yellows.

Her grandiose jewelry
is mosaic gold and silver.

Driven to novelty—
she and Phillip are outside
the chapel chatting.

He still loves her lips, smiling lips:
a glowing brightness.
Although he wants to kiss her
instead he congratulates her.

In any case, a kiss might unbalance
her headgear,
a Byzantine vastness.

Inside, her husband-to-be
is waiting at the altar.
Not to keep him waiting,
Phillip does the honorable thing.

Eye Wash

Men pushing wheelbarrows
of potatoes and rice
from deck to land.
Sacks of beets and sacks of barley
down the plank onto the dock.
— — —

The Apocalypse in smoke.
Tanner at his easel.
Bonnard's mistress,
Renee—dead in a hotel room.
— — —

The greenhouse.
The pavilion.
The bandstand.
The coffee shop is open
till ten tonight.
The coffee shop workers
with their aprons
stained with coffee, vanilla,
and powered sugar.
— — —

Women from next door
wearing aprons—
as if they've just stepped out
of the kitchen to cut the rug a bit.

— — —

The blue peacock got out again.
He walks between the dull-green hedges
trimmed beautifully, skillfully sculpted.
They seem to shield him
from imaginary predators.

He stops at the fork in the road,
pink under sunlight,
apparently unsure of which way to go.
He actively looks back for a long minute,
over the expanse of his long tail.

— — —

Grinning, Peg Leg Bates is doing splits.
He taps around in a circle
and does another split.
And another one.

— — —

A robin near her nest

high in a tree.

She flies away then returns

with a worm

hanging from her mouth

She feeds her young.

She starts her angry thrush song

of private space,

saying you are too close.

— — —

The yellow lick of early spring,

the deep and tall green of summer,

the yellow oxide of winter,

spin together in a wistful whirl.

— — —

On the playground

a boy asked to see

my toy truck.

I took it from my pocket.

He snatched it and ran.

— — —

The Pagoda teahouse.

The taiko bashi (Drum Bridge).
The precision of the waterfall
and the water flowing down
The shrubbery and the plants.
The yin-yang arrangement.
The circle of the dwarf cherry trees.
The line of magnolia.
The square of the camellia trees.
The profusion of dwarf maples.
The tallness of the pine trees.
The lovely cedars
and the magestic cypresses.
The bubbling sounds of water
streaming over smooth rocks.

My Studio

More than you would think
can happen in this limited space.
Spatial compression has its virtues.

The easel stands tall and books line the wall.
Start with a counterpoint then embellish.

It's a visual metaphor, a working space,
soaked in bright north light.

This is where I respect a certain aesthetic,
an interior with a motive,
explore the geometry of images,
where I investigate immediacy,
emulate my ideal,
frolic with new ideas,
retouch the touchable,
and make myths of myself enraptured.

A room of one's own?
This is more than a room.
It's an unimpeded mental vista.

CPSIA information can be obtained
at www.ICGtesting.com
Printed in the USA
LVHW09s0552210918
590894LV00001B/161/P